MAY 17 1994

DULUTH PUBLIC LIBRARY
520 WEST SUPERIOR STREET
DULUTH, MINNESOTA 55802

WITHDRAWN

Charles Proteus Steinmetz, mathematician and electrical engineer, was born in Breslau, Germany. Although physically deformed from birth, Steinmetz was otherwise a normally bright, inquisitive child. He fled Germany for political reasons in the late 1880's, coming to America where he became known as the "Wizard of Light" for his astounding and original experiments with lightning and electrical currents. Steinmetz's discovery of laws governing the use of alternating current makes possible our present use of electrical equipment and machinery.

Steinmetz: Wizard of Light

Steinmetz: Wizard of Light

Anne Welsh Guy

Illustrated by Leonard Rosoman

Alfred A. Knopf: New York

L.C. Catalog card number: 65-21565

THIS IS A BORZOI BOOK, PUBLISHED BY ALFRED A. KNOPF, INC.

Copyright © 1965 by Anne Welsh Guy
All rights reserved. No part of this book may be reproduced in any form without permission in writing from the publisher, except by a reviewer, who may quote brief passages and reproduce not more than three illustrations in a review to be printed in a magazine or newspaper. Manufactured in the United States of America, and distributed by Random House, Inc. Published simultaneously in Toronto, Canada, by Random House of Canada, Limited.

JUVENILE

921
St36g
Copy 1

*To my son, Richard Guy,
and his wife, Shirley Ann.*

Acknowledgment

The author wishes to make acknowledgment to the following individuals for their cooperation and assistance.

To Dr. and Mrs. Simon Nathan for background material on Charles Steinmetz's early life in Breslau, Germany.

To Dr. R. J. Seegur of the National Science Foundation, who checked the manuscript for scientific accuracy.

To Mrs. Bessie White, whose critical analysis and interest went far beyond the usual editorial assistance.

And to my typist, Mrs. Ira Shimasaki, for invaluable secretarial services.

Contents

1: *A Small Boy Experiments* 3

2: *Troubles at School* 11

3: *A Great Disappointment* 24

4: *College Days* 34

5: *Escape* 42

6: *America!* 51

7: *First Discovery* 60

8: *New Way of Life* 68

9: *Family Man* 76

10: *Years of Glory* 84

11: *Dreams Come True* 94

Steinmetz: Wizard of Light

✳ 1

A Small Boy Experiments

It was the year 1870 in the old city of Breslau, Germany. In the kitchen of a little flat, Grandmother Steinmetz was making strudel. A train, belching smoke and cinders, shook the walls of the shabby wooden building.

"Trains are so noisy and dirty," grumbled the woman.

She paused and sniffed the air. "Something is

Steinmetz: *Wizard of Light*

burning. I smell it. And it is not train smoke." Wiping her hands, she ran to the little room at the end of the hall. "Oh, Karl," she cried.

Smoke rose from the carpet while a small boy stamped among the wooden blocks scattered at his feet. A candle lay there, dripping wax.

The child turned in fright. "Fire out, Grandmother. It only burned a little hole. I put it out."

"My beautiful carpet!" Angrily, the grandmother began to gather up the blocks. "Karl, you make so much trouble. If only your father would punish you. What were you doing?"

With a scream, the boy threw himself to the floor and beat his head against it. "I—b—built a temple," he sobbed. "With many rooms, like King Solomon's in the Bible. It was dark in the temple, so I made a light for the soldiers. Then a train came by and shook everything. The candle fell down and burned the carpet. The train did it, Grandmother."

"It is done already, Karl. No use crying now. But you are too small to make a fire. Next time you need light, tell me."

A Small Boy Experiments

Karl smiled through the tears. His homely little face brightened. He threw both arms about his grandmother's neck.

"Don't tell Father. PLEASE!" he begged.

"Then tell him yourself. Now put back the blocks and wash. Your sisters will be coming from school soon. Maybe they will take you to the duck pond."

When Mr. Steinmetz returned from his office in the railroad yard, no little boy waited at the door as usual. Karl was in the corner of the small room at the end of the hall waiting for his father to see the rug.

The man's troubled eyes were only for his child. Quickly, he picked up Karl. It was a twisted little figure he held, with spindly, crooked legs and hair falling about a head too big for the frail body. There was an ugly hump on the little back. "What is wrong, Karlchen?"

Karl rested his face against his father's. The man carried him to a chair and held him on his lap as the boy poured out his story.

"You were brave to put the fire out quickly,"

his father said. "I am not angry. I am proud of you."

Happily, Karl slid down and hobbled to the kitchen. "Grandmother, Clara, Marie!" he cried in a high little voice. "Father is not angry. He is proud of me."

His sisters, helping to prepare supper, looked fondly at the boy. He stood awkwardly in the doorway, and Marie dropped on her knees to hug him. "Funny little Karl," she said comfortingly.

After the children were in bed, the grandmother took up her knitting. She sat beside her son who was reading the newspaper. "Karl, it would be better to punish the boy, so that he may never again make a fire when he is alone. He could burn the house down!"

"He likes to do experiments, Mother. Remarkable for a child not yet five years old!"

"Experiments!" Grandmother wailed. "Yesterday, it was a water wheel. To make it turn, he poured water over it and onto my rug. His experiments could become dangerous. Put him in

A Small Boy Experiments

a school, my son, where they could watch him."

Throwing down the newspaper, Mr. Steinmetz rose and limped back and forth across the room without speaking. He paused to gaze into a cloudy mirror over a cheap sideboard. In it he saw a small man, with his head sunk into his shoulders, and deep-set gloomy eyes. He looked down at his own slight figure and at his short, uneven legs.

"Mother, my son looks like me. How can he have a good life?" The man threw himself into a chair. "If Karl's mother had not died when he was a year old, it might have been different. I could bear to be more strict. But how can I punish a motherless, humpbacked dwarf who faces many problems in life. God be thanked he learns so fast."

They remained silent for a time. Then a smile came to man's sad face. "Karl needs more than blocks. He has a birthday soon. Mother, leave it all to me." He kissed her plump cheek.

Little Karl rose at six o'clock on the morning of

A Small Boy Experiments

his fifth birthday. There, by his cereal bowl, lay a large package. The eager boy tore off the paper and uncovered a bright red locomotive. "Father, Father, it is your present! Will it run like a big train? Show me how, Father, please. Quick, Father!"

"Yes, Karlchen, it runs. But only a fire makes it work."

Mr. Steinmetz took the locomotive in his hands. He got down on the floor beside Karl. "You may not have it until you make a promise."

"Yes, yes, Father. I will do anything you tell me."

"It is what you must *not* do, Karl. Promise never to make a fire when you are alone."

"I promise, Father, never to make a fire when I am alone."

So, Mr. Steinmetz showed Karl how to start the engine. First, water in the boiler. Then, a match. Carefully, he lighted the wick of the wood alcohol container beneath the boiler. Karl, speechless with delight, watched as the water turned into steam, and wheels began to turn.

Steinmetz: *Wizard of Light*

"It goes, Father! All by itself!"

"Yes, Karl, it can go anywhere on the floor because it has no tracks to run on. Play with it only when Grandmother is watching."

When his father came home from work, he brought a second package. "I sent to Berlin for this, Karl. It is for you and for the whole family. It will surprise many people here in Breslau, too."

The family gasped in amazement when they saw what was in the second package—a magnificent kerosene lamp with two wicks! Few people in all of Germany, in that time of candles and whale oil, had even seen such a thing! Karl watched eagerly as both great wicks were lighted. Father placed the big lamp by the window that evening. People stopped to stare and to marvel.

What a bright stream of light poured into the dark street! Like a beacon! Karl sat in the window beside it, fascinated by this second wonder that came to him in one day! In bed that night, he could not fall asleep. Lights, flames, wheels! They flashed and danced before him as he lay awake, wondering and thinking. It was almost morning before his eyes closed.

✸ 2
Troubles at School

The good smell of sauerkraut and potato dumplings filled the little flat. Grandmother was in the kitchen. Father sat alone, close by a window in the small alcove. He tried to read by the last glimmer of daylight but it was too dark.

Rising, he lit the wicks in the great lamp. The room was a strange sight. Overturned tables and chairs were placed about on the floor. In a corner stood Karl's locomotive. Around it were several wooden cars that he had made for Karl.

"Come, Mother, come," Father called. "Sit with me until the children get here. Let us talk."

Grandmother came to the door. *"Sit* you tell me! Where shall I sit? This home is only a train yard for Karl. All day I stumble over furniture and hear orders, "A match, Grandmother! Alcohol for my train! And a light! Help me turn over the table and chairs for my stations!'"

The man patted her hand. "At least, Mother, the boy no longer burns holes in your carpet."

"My carpet! Can I see it, with furniture all over it? The boy is a little tyrant. If I move a chair or touch his train he starts screaming. Karl, I insist something should be done!"

Loud noises outside silenced her. The front door was flung open as Clara and Marie pulled their brother into the house.

"Father!" Marie cried. "We shall never take Karl to the duck pond again."

"We were ashamed of him," Clara added. "He is a bad boy."

Troubles at School

Once inside, Karl paid no further attention to anyone. He hobbled toward his train in the corner and crouched beside it.

"We played games," went on Clara, "with Karl and a little girl and boy. Karl wanted to win. The little girl could skip better, so Karl pushed her down in the dirt. The boy could catch the ball and Karl couldn't, so he wouldn't play ball. When the children sailed boats, Karl started his boat ahead, to reach the other side of the pond first. We tried to help him win, but soon we had to drag him home. He fought us all the way, and everyone looked at us! We were ashamed!"

Karl paid no attention to all this. "Choo-choooooo, Ch-ch-chooo!" Karl steered his train by hand at great speed around furniture and toward the feet of the sisters.

"Karl, you hurt me," cried Clara, as the train struck her legs.

He was aiming at Marie when his father scooped him up in his arms. Setting a chair upright, he sat down with his son. "We don't want

Troubles at School

to be ashamed of our Karl," he said. "You are right, Mother. It *is* time for him to go to school. He will become a scholar, and make us proud."

The little body stiffened, the dark eyes widened with fear. Karl looked into the faces around him.

Grandmother spoke firmly. "Yes, Karl, you should become a scholar. You need not stay all day with only a grandmother for company."

Tears began to roll down Karl's cheeks. At once, the girls dropped by his side to comfort him. "Don't cry, Karlchen," Marie said. "You will go with me. Your kindergarten is near my school. I will take care of you."

"There will be games to play," Clara added, "with other children, too. You will have fun."

Questioningly, Karl looked into his father's face. He saw only an encouraging smile. "Yes, Karl, there will be a good teacher who will like you and be kind. At noon, when I come home for lunch, you can tell me what has happened at school. Behave well now, and go with your sisters tomorrow."

Steinmetz: Wizard of Light

The next noon, Mr. Steinmetz hurried home. Not only Karl and the girls awaited him. A serious young woman was there, too. Marie introduced Miss Mueller, the kindergarten teacher, who spoke firmly.

"Mr. Steinmetz, we cannot keep your boy. He caused trouble all morning, beating his head on the floor and screaming. We had to send for Marie to come and quiet him. He is too young for school. Better keep him home a year longer."

Miss Mueller left and the girls hurried off to the kitchen. Karl's face beamed with joy and satisfaction. Mr. Steinmetz, a troubled look in his eyes, sank into a chair. After a time, Karl edged over and slipped a hand into his father's.

Smiling up at him, he said comfortingly, "Next year I will go to school, Father—if you want me to. I *will* go—a long, long time from now," he added hopefully.

"Attention, boys!" The headmaster of the first primary group class at St. John's School for Boys rapped on his desk. "Today, the first primary group will prepare the seven times table." He was talking to the seven and eight-year-old boys. Then he spoke to the older boys of nine and ten. "Second primary group will repeat Latin verbs. I expect a perfect recitation from all of you."

As he said these words, Mr. Schmidt turned and looked directly at the smallest boy in the room. It was Karl Steinmetz, now seven years old. He sat on the front bench, his feet hanging uncomfortably several inches from the floor. Boys looked over at him and grinned. Hastily, he opened an arithmetic study book and bent over the multiplication tables. "7 × 1 is 7," he whispered to himself. "7 × 2 is 14, 7 × 3 is...."

Boys droning Latin verbs distracted his attention. He covered his ears with his hands and turned his head to look out the window. Lightning darted across the pane above him. Then came a thunder clap. Karl forgot the seven times table. What makes thunder, he wondered, and lightning? How does it leap across the sky? Why does silver rain come down? Why? Why? He leaned forward to see the sky more clearly.

Steinmetz: *Wizard of Light*

"Karl Steinmetz!" The stern voice brought Karl back to the schoolroom. "Repeat the seven times table." The boy slid to the floor. Someone snickered and Mr. Schmidt rapped angrily.

"I—I—I forgot, sir. I forgot to learn it."

"You forgot. Why do you always forget to learn in school?"

Karl looked down at his feet, his face red with shame. "I—I d-don't know wh-why."

"Well, I *do* know why." Mr. Schmidt wrote hastily on a sheet of paper. "And it is time your father knew why, too." He slipped the paper into an envelope, sealed it with wax, and handed it to Karl. "Give this to your father. Tell him to come here to see me before eight o'clock tomorrow morning."

Karl sank on his bench. He made no attempt to study. He did not leave the bench until four o'clock, when school was over. He hardly heard boys reciting pages of Latin and rules of algebra. During the twenty minute lunch period, he did not eat the black bread, yellow cheese, and apple strudel in his lunch box. When the boys went

Troubles at School

out at three o'clock for games, he did not join them.

"The hunchback has a hump on his back," a boy called out. "A twist in the head, too." He made a circle with his finger on his forehead. All the boys laughed.

No one befriended the crippled boy who sat with his head on his arms. But a man passing the schoolroom door stopped and looked in at him—a tall, gray-haired man with a pointed gray beard. Finally, he went away. But, when Karl's father came to school next morning, the man was standing beside Mr. Schmidt.

The teacher introduced the stranger. "Professor Fechner, who has been teaching the upper classes here for many years wishes to meet you, Mr. Steinmetz." After the men shook hands, the teacher went on. "I'm sorry to say that your son Karl is stupid. He cannot even learn the multiplication tables."

Though the day was cool, the father mopped his face with a big handkerchief.

"Karl needs a special school or lessons at

home," the teacher continued. "He does not fit in here with boys preparing for a university, perhaps to be world leaders."

Mr. Steinmetz replied sadly, "I cannot understand it. At home, Karl learns very fast."

"What does the boy learn so fast at home?" Professor Fechner asked. "What interests him?"

"He is always experimenting and his mind is full of ideas. Lightning, what is it and why? Can he make it himself? He asks many such questions, Professor. But I have little learning and cannot answer him."

The professor's eyes gleamed. "So-o-o-o. The same thoughts filled my mind when I was his age." Then he smiled. "Perhaps we are worrying too much about young Karl."

But Karl's father was not comforted. One who cannot even learn the multiplication tables will amount to little in life, he thought. A cripple who is stupid as well; what will become of him?

Aloud he said, "Karl will trouble you no further, sir. He will learn at home." With a heavy

Troubles at School

heart, Mr. Steinmetz left for his day's work.

That evening, Grandmother met him at the door. "Sh— sh—. Come to the kitchen with me. A man is talking to Karl—for a long time now—behind a closed door."

Karl had been frightened when Professor Fechner came to call, but a kindly smile put him at his ease. Now, they were still talking. "I have been thinking about you, Karlchen, and how much you are like me when I was a boy."

Karl was so amazed that he lost his shyness. He stared up at the tall, fine-looking man. "But —P-Professor Fechner, excuse me please. How can that be?" The boy looked down at his own twisted legs.

"I speak of the mind, Karl—not the legs. I hear you want to be a scientist—to experiment and invent."

"Yes, Professor Fechner. But how can I learn to become a scientist? In school, there are only tables, verbs, and pages to memorize. I cannot ask questions. No one wishes to tell me why or to show me how."

"Are the multiplication tables so hard, Karl, that you cannot memorize them?"

"No, not too hard. But there is so much more to think about, and school is noisy. Besides, no one there likes me." He looked into Professor Fechner's eyes timidly and saw understanding and interest in them.

Professor Fechner pulled a book out of his pocket and turned the pages quickly. "Here, Karl, show me if you can learn the seven times table." Excitement came into Karl's eyes. He bent over the book and, for a few moments, the only sound was the big clock ticking.

Very soon, the boy looked up. Quickly and perfectly, he repeated the table. Professor Fechner threw back his head and laughed. "I knew you could do it, Karl! You can learn what any bright seven or eight-year-old can. While the others play, you are able to learn quickly. Like a true scientist, you will find out the secrets of nature. You can experiment and prove your experiments. If you do these things, you will make people proud to know you."

Karl's eyes glowed. "Professor Fechner, you be my teacher! Please, please!" he begged.

"In the fifth class group you will study with me, Karl. When you are a big boy, four years from now, I shall be waiting. Until then, come and talk with me whenever you wish. I am your friend."

His father could not believe his eyes when he and Grandmother came to bid the visitor good night. What a change in Karl! The boy held the Professor's hand, his dark eyes shining.

"Your son is to return to school in the morning," said Professor Fechner, smiling. "He promises to study hard. Every person should have a second chance. Is that not so, my friend?" he asked gently, looking down into Karl's radiant face.

3 ✳

A Great Disappointment

There was excitement in the air at St. John's School for Boys. It was a Saturday noon in April of 1882, one week before graduation. Seventeen-year-old Karl Steinmetz was to be one of the graduates. For five days, he had been writing examination papers. Now, he had finished the last one. He walked past the groups of boys and started toward home.

A Great Disappointment

During the years at St. John's, he had kept his promise to Professor Fechner. He had gone back to school on that day, nine years ago, with a new plan for life. He would do well in *all* his lessons. No more daydreaming. His progress began to amaze everyone, even himself.

By the time he was ten years old, the crippled boy led his class. Latin, Greek, French, Polish, Hebrew, algebra, and geometry were the subjects the boys studied. Karl mastered them all. Mathematics was easiest for him and the subject he liked best. He grasped rules and principles immediately. Problems that the class took hours to solve on paper, he worked out in his head almost instantly.

Karl enjoyed St. John's and was pleased with his progress. Each long talk with Professor Fechner made him more ambitious. But he was not completely happy.

Often, he gazed through the open door to the playground, filled with laughing, shouting boys. He longed to leave his books and become one of them. But, when he tried to join their games, they did not welcome him. If only just once, one boy would shout, "I choose Karl—I want Karl on my side." No one ever did.

"Forget your handicaps," Professor Fechner told him. "The mind is what counts. You are a genius." Karl wished he could exchange that genius for a strong, healthy body.

Now he was to graduate from the Gymnasium —the High School—a very great honor in those days when few boys finished school or went to a university. Karl knew he had done well in all his studies. He felt tired that day but happy, as he limped down the street toward home. He was also a bit sad.

If Grandmother were alive, she would be so proud to see me graduate, he thought. And if only Clara and Marie could leave their good jobs in the big city and return home for one evening. All the boys have families who will see them honored. I have only Father.

Mr. Steinmetz waited at the flat, a smile on his face and a lunch basket in his hand. "Karl, I have taken this afternoon off from work. We

A Great Disappointment

will walk to the woods and relax. It will clear our minds and we can make plans for you—for after graduation." Karl agreed readily, for he was fond of the outdoors and of hiking.

Finally, reaching a pleasant hilltop, they sat down and began to talk. "First about graduation night," said Karl, biting into a sausage, "it will cost too much money."

"Son?" Mr. Steinmetz glanced at the boy's worried face.

"Yes—the dress suit, with tail coat, stiff shirt, white tie, top hat. We must have all that to take oral examinations. Only if a boy is on the Honor Roll can he escape oral examination for the diploma. But that will not happen to anyone in my class."

To Karl's surprise, his father's sober face broke into a smile. "Karl, I know all this. Why did you not speak of it sooner? I want you to be like the rest. I will manage to buy all that you need. Our friend, the tailor, can make it all fit in time."

A feeling of contentment stole over Karl. A dress suit like the rest! That would be good. He stretched out under a tree and gazed at the glinting waters of the Oder River, as it wound its way through the town below.

"What are your plans, Karl? Will you become an engineer at the railroad yards? You always liked trains, and you would be well paid."

"Yes, I have always wanted to find out what makes things run," said Karl smiling. "When I was little, I often sat in your office and watched the trains rush by. After graduation, shall I run a train or maybe work with you in the office?"

His father shook his head. "Karl, you must not be a clerk like me. Nor should you run a train! You can be something much higher!" He laid a hand gently on Karl's shoulder. "One thing we do know. A boy with your brain must go on to a university."

Karl's eyes misted with tears. "Father, you cannot pay for six more years of study. Where will the money come from?"

"As we will find money for a dress suit, so we can find money for a university. I will pay some; you can earn by tutoring younger boys."

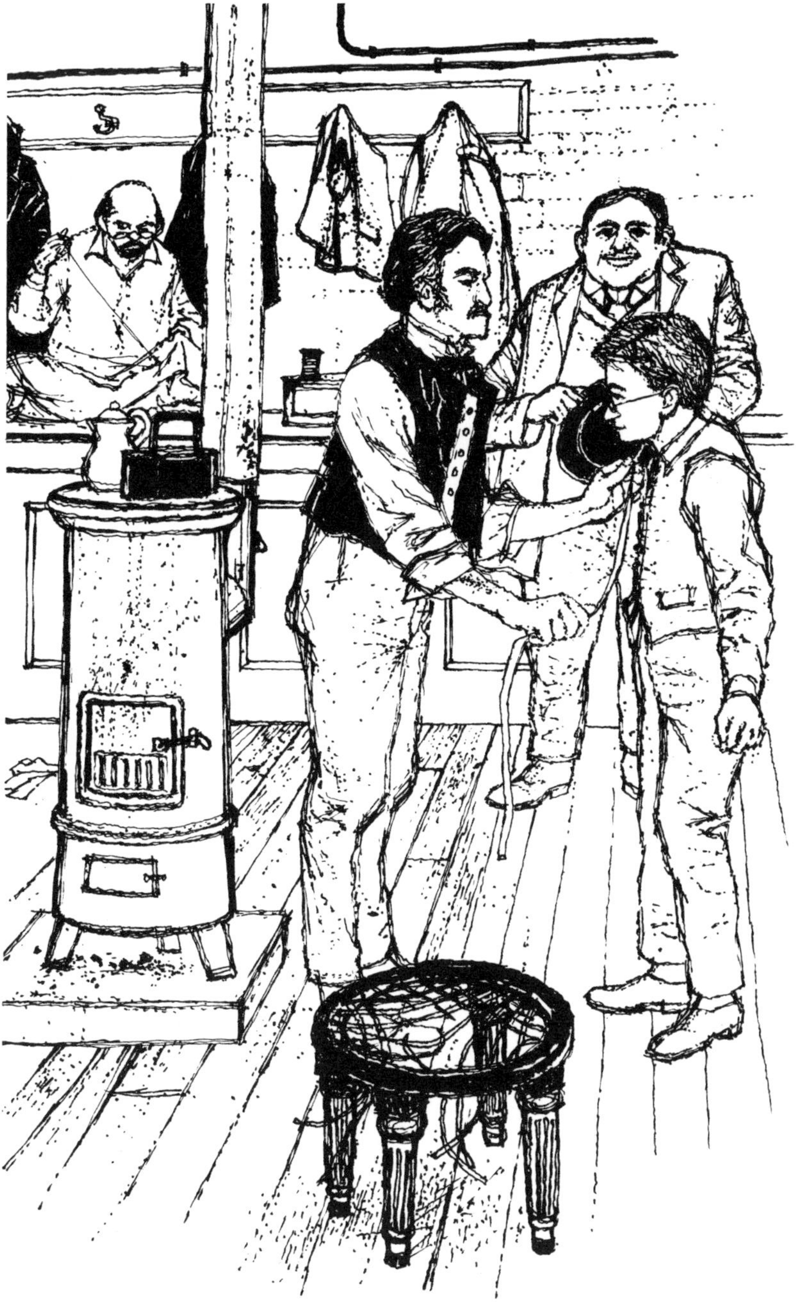

He gave Karl a poke in the ribs. "First, we must go to buy the dress suit."

It was almost closing time at the shop when they arrived and the tailor was anxious to go home. He looked at Karl's wide shoulders, crooked legs, and the ugly hump on his back. "It will take too much altering to make any suit in my shop fit you," he grumbled. "A boy only four feet tall will look too comical." Seeing the hurt in Karl's eyes, the man spoke more kindly. "But I will try."

Proudly, Karl hung the dress suit away. He could hardly wait to wear it at graduation. What excitement there would be! As each boy walked out on the platform, he must really "think on his feet," while family and friends listened eagerly. Difficult questions were asked, and no boy got a diploma unless he gave perfect answers. Wearing that dress suit, Karl was confident that he would do well.

Whistling merrily, he shuffled across the schoolyard to his locker. In it were books and

A Great Disappointment

notes he needed. In the halls, noisy boys milled about. As he entered, one boy shouted, "Come see what's on the bulletin board!" Excited boys stopped talking and made way for Karl.

Under the heading, *Honor Roll,* there was only one name:

KARL AUGUST RUDOLPH STEINMETZ

Then in small print:

For exceptional scholarship,
No oral examinations.

Stunned, Karl read the words over and over. They meant not being on the platform with the rest! Not wearing a tail coat! Not receiving a diploma to wild applause! With a lump in his throat, he turned to go.

A boy called after him, "Lucky Steinmetz, no oral exams."

"No wearing a silly monkey suit," cried another.

"A lot they know about me," thought Karl, holding back tears. He went straight home to the closet. Quickly, he packed away the suit, climbed on a stool, and pushed the box far back on a shelf.

Father was told the news that night. Seeing the pain in his son's eyes, he hid his own grief and made an effort to sound calm. "A great honor, my Karl. Such a thing has not happened in many years at St. John's. Tomorrow morning, we will get your diploma from the school. That alone is important since it is for all your life. Graduation exercises are only for one evening."

At the exercises the next night, Mr. Steinmetz and Karl, in his cheap brown suit, listened and watched. Professor Fechner read Karl's name. "The only one who made the Honor Roll," he explained. There was applause. Then boys came proudly to the platform, to receive honors and applause. Karl hated it all. Is this how I must be, he thought bitterly—sitting apart, being different? Will all my life be this way?

At home, he announced to his father, "I shall never in my whole life wear a dress suit." Father put his hand on the boy's shoulder. "My Karl, you cannot run away from your body. You and

I have humps on our backs. Many people have humps that do not show. Just go through the life ahead of you in good spirit, with high accomplishment."

Karl pondered these words in bed that night. His anger melted, his spirits lifted. After all, I did get the highest honor, he thought, as he drifted into a sound sleep.

4 ✳

College Days

Voices of students, singing a German college song, rang out. It was almost midnight. They walked, arm in arm, through the hushed streets of Breslau, toward an inn outside the town. Among them, a queer little figure shuffled and sang lustily.

Near the Ring, in the center of town, they grew quiet. By the many-towered Town Hall

College Days

they had spied "The Watch," swinging a lantern and holding a horn. He blew a shrill blast. "Hear, hear," he cried. "Twelve o'clock. Midnight. Close your doors and sleep in peace."

The boys filed by quietly, but burst into song again when beyond his hearing. Lights from the inn gleamed at the top of a steep, narrow, cobblestone street.

"Tonight I treat," shouted Karl. Laughing, shouting, noisy, they climbed the pavement and pushed through the door. A student snatched the colored cap from Karl's head, which "foxes" or first year students wore, and threw it into the air. "Proteus pays," he cried.

The innkeeper, in his huge, white apron, bustled toward them, past tables with blue checked cloths. "Good! If Karl does not have enough, I will help him pay. No one leaves my inn hungry."

"Good fellow," shouted the students. "Always food—money or not. So, we always come here."

When the innkeeper served Karl a stein of beer and a thick sandwich, he asked, "Why do they call you Proteus now?"

"They named me that at my initiation into the Math Society." Karl laughed. "Homer wrote about Proteus in the Greek Myths. He lived in the River Nile. An ugly, humpbacked dwarf like me."

A tall, blond fellow leaned over to Karl and clapped him on the shoulder. "Yes, Karl, you are like Proteus! You know all the answers to all questions."

Another raised his stein. "A toast! A toast, everyone! Proteus, old man of the sea, could change instantly from lion to sea serpent, from tiger to blazing fire. Our Karl is like that. His mind is so quick, we cannot catch up with it."

All rose as if pulled by a string, and they raised their steins high. "To Proteus! We have him and will try to keep him until he gives us all the answers of the universe."

Karl's face beamed. The boys sat down and fell to eating with noisy pleasure. After more singing, joking, and laughter, they rose to go home.

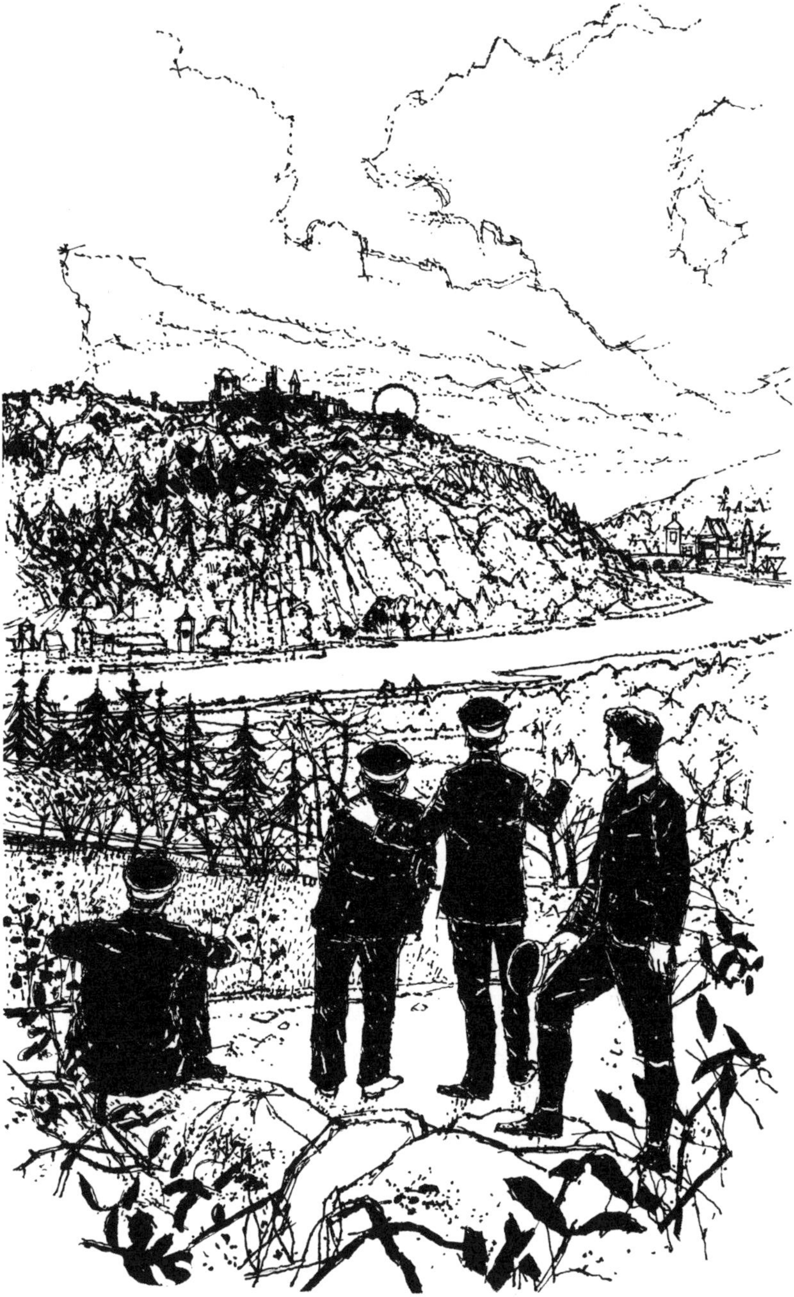

"Watch the sun rise with me," challenged Karl. How could he bear to let an exciting, happy night end now? With a few friends, he hiked off under a black sky filled with stars. Through the Ring, across the big stone bridge, into the countryside. Taking deep breaths of the frosty autumn air, they tramped through open fields, through pine woods, and up a hillside. The sun rising over the Oder River outlined the ancient, castlelike University in the early morning light. When belfry chimes in the old stone cathedral began to ring out, they started home.

Farm animals stirred in the barnyards. Early-rising peasants were on their way to market in wagons filled with late potatoes. As the sun spilled its light over the city, the boys separated and went wearily toward their homes.

Only Karl did not go to bed that Saturday morning. Mr. Steinmetz, coming from his bedroom and rubbing sleep from his eyes, saw the boy at the sink, dousing his face with cold water. "A long night for you, my son. What happened at the meeting?"

College Days

"I must hurry. Good lectures today, Father. We will talk tonight, please." Picking up a thick black notebook, Karl grabbed his colored cap and hobbled away.

Mr. Steinmetz sat with his son among a cluttered collection of beakers, batteries, and test tubes. They were in the room where Karl had played as a child. It was now a laboratory where he could work and study while at college. The University had one huge building on the river, and no campus. Other classrooms were in buildings throughout the town. There were no study halls or dormitories. Boys lived and studied in their homes or in rented rooms.

Karl's father proudly ruffled the pages of the thick, black notebook which he held. "So many notes! Karl, why do you take more courses than others do?"

Karl, busy sticking copper wires into a pot of white paste, did not seem to hear.

"I am experimenting, Father, with the action of electric current in making metal."

Steinmetz: *Wizard of Light*

Mr. Steinmetz peered into the pot and saw only a salty-looking mixture. "That will be a metal?" he asked, puzzled.

"Perhaps...." Karl replied excitedly. "Perhaps it will be the metal of the future. I shall experiment with it."

His father turned back to the notebook. "Why do you study by yourself day and night, Karl? You make endless experiments like this one. You write pages and pages of calculations. No one at the University keeps track of you. No recitations. No examinations. Who knows if you attend lectures or not? Why do you do all this—why?"

Karl dropped into a chair beside his father. "A wonderful place—the University of Breslau, Father. Teachers come only to *teach*. Students come to *learn,* and only those who have learned may graduate. I want to learn it all. I cannot decide what to choose so I must try everything —chemistry, medicine, engineering. Shall I be a scientist? Or a professor? The students here have good times along with their work. Also, they like

College Days

and respect me—they even admire me, Father! Perhaps I will stay here with you and my friends and teach mathematics at the University. Mathematics I *do* like!" Karl returned to his experiment.

"Yes, Karl, you *do* like mathematics." His father smiled. "Numbers are a game for you."

Numbers ran through Karl's head constantly. He juggled them and played with them. Already, this first year, he was far ahead of his class, taking the most advanced courses. His exceptional memory and agile mind worked like magic. He needed only to close his eyes for a moment when given a complicated problem. Presto! The answer. No pencil or paper was needed.

The world of study remained gay and exciting to him throughout his university years. Acceptance into the Math Society made him very happy for he enjoyed parties, liked people, and was always hoping to make new friends. But, during his fifth year, he joined another society. This step brought serious trouble upon him, and it changed his whole life.

5 ✻

Escape

It was June of 1888. A celebration went on in the small back room with the black curtain over the door. The room was the office of a newspaper published by the Socialist Club of Breslau. Karl Steinmetz was a member of the club and one of the two editors of its paper.

This group was part of a movement that began about ten years earlier. By now, it had spread all over Europe. The Socialists aimed for complete freedom for all and a better life for the working class. Most students and thinking people were concerned with these problems.

The Breslau Socialist Club did not believe in war. They were against Bismark, the German Chancellor, and his army, who were trying to take over Germany and make it the most powerful country in the world. Karl loved Germany and he wanted it to be democratic. He wanted more freedom for all Germans to think for themselves; to express their thoughts freely in the press. For this reason he had become editor of a newspaper, *The People's Voice,* that opposed the government.

Bismark was anxious to destroy all Socialist newspapers and to wipe out Socialist clubs. Karl's co-editor, one of his fellow students—Heinrich Lux—had been jailed. Karl took his place, and now the police were keeping a close watch on him. The release of Lux after ten months in jail was one reason for the celebration. The approach of graduation was another.

Karl's thesis was written. He would get a degree of Doctor of Philosophy and graduate with highest honors. A post at the University of Breslau as Professor of Mathematics waited for him. He and his friends had gathered to celebrate.

"Karl, you made it possible for me to graduate." Lux put his arm around Karl's shoulders. "I could not have finished my thesis alone, nor worked toward my release. Your notes in invisible ink on the pages of the books you sent to me in jail really did it. How can I ever thank you?"

Karl laughed. "Lucky we figured out in chemistry class that mixing permanganate of potash in mouthwash, with toilet water, makes a colorless ink. The prison guards were easy to fool. They searched the pages of our books but saw nothing. And you supplied the heat to make the notes readable."

Hearing this, another student warned, "The police and the government may not always be fooled as easily."

But Karl was too happy to worry over the future. "A song for old time's sake," he cried.

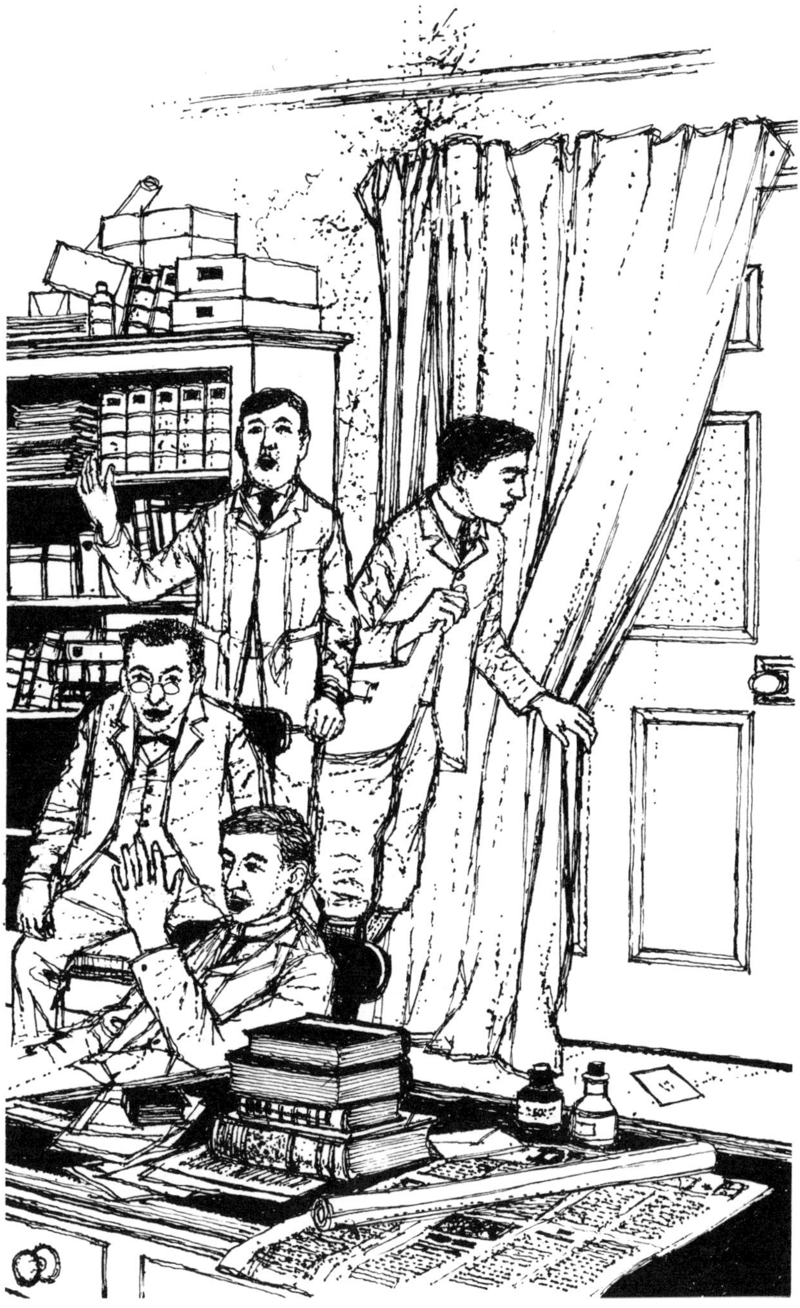

"The police cannot object to that."

Through all this, a friend noticed a white paper being slipped under the curtain at the door. He picked it up and cried, "Hear this!"

> *"Karl, if you want to save yourself, get out of Germany tonight or you will be arrested tomorrow and thrown into jail. Destroy this note.*
> *A friend on the Breslau faculty."*

Karl's face grew white. He imagined himself being dragged by policemen to a jail cell, to stay in solitary confinement for many months. There was a buzz of excitement as Lux brought Karl's shabby overcoat and helped him into it. "On your way, friend," he urged.

"Cross the border into Switzerland," another advised. "You can make it to safety before morning."

The men crowded about, thumping Karl on the shoulder, shaking his hand. Out into the night and through the dark streets of Breslau he half walked, half ran. Back at the flat, he threw

Escape

into a bag his best suit, a few shirts, a few books, and a bulky manuscript—his thesis. Last of all, he stuffed in a small, battered, red locomotive.

He tiptoed to his father's door, thinking, "Again, I must cause him disappointment." There was pain in the blue eyes behind the heavy, steel-rimmed glasses as he gently roused the man.

"Father, I am going away on a visit."

"Have a good time, my boy." Father turned over and fell asleep, never to see his son again.

The towers of the town hall in the Ring, silhouetted against the night sky, looked cold and unfriendly as Karl boarded a train on the railroad his father had served so long.

One year later, in a cheap bedroom in Zurich, Switzerland, Karl sat cross-legged on a chair. He read a letter written in small, careful handwriting which said:

"I miss you, son. But to return to Germany means arrest and prison. Your opinions are known. Better stay where you are. It is good you were accepted at the University

there. It is good you get money from your scientific writings, even though it is little money. Stay and live where men think and speak freely."

A familiar whistle sounded on the stairs and Oscar Asmussen burst in. He was a tall, fair-skinned Danish boy whose home was in America with an uncle. His uncle had sent him to be educated in Zurich, where he had met Karl. They became roommates and great friends. Now Oscar's face was red and angry. He, too, held a letter which he waved in Karl's face.

"From my uncle in San Francisco," he cried, speaking in German. "He sends money for a first class ticket to America. He demands that I return at once, and he forbids my marriage to my Swiss sweetheart. I refuse to obey. Besides, I have not finished my studies." Oscar pounded the table with his big fist, then dropped to a chair, head in hands. At last, he spoke despairingly. "What else can I do? I am dependent on him so I must go back. But I shall send for my sweet-

Escape

heart. It will not take long to earn her passage money. I shall get a job of my own in New York."

"Is it so easy to earn money in America?" Karl asked.

Asmussen sprang up, eyes lighting with enthusiasm. "Anyone can make a living there, Karl. Come, join me on the voyage back. Trained scientists are badly needed in America."

Karl shook his head. He pulled out a handful of coins. "Hardly enough to eat after our rent is paid."

Asmussen looked serious, then suddenly brightened. "I have it. One first class passage will pay for two steerage tickets. Karl, my friend, we go steerage—you and I—I insist!"

Excitement overwhelmed Karl as Oscar rushed off to his sweetheart. America! The very word inspired him. Surely a place, as Father said, where men think freely. A place where all are alike and where all can earn a good living. A hunchback, too, would be welcome there. Even as a child, Karl had dreamed of going to America. Now his chance had come! To see the cities, the factories, the fabulous Brooklyn Bridge.

Steinmetz: *Wizard of Light*

Heart thumping, he slid down from the chair. With shaking hands, he began to gather together his few belongings.

✻ 6

America!

The small, dark, steerage deck on the prow of the French ship, *La Champagne,* was crowded with passengers. Greeks, Slavs, Italians, Serbians—men, women, and children. It had been a stormy eight days. The ocean, filled with wrath, had tossed and rocked the ship about like a toy. Karl had expected to enjoy the voyage. How different it had turned out to be!

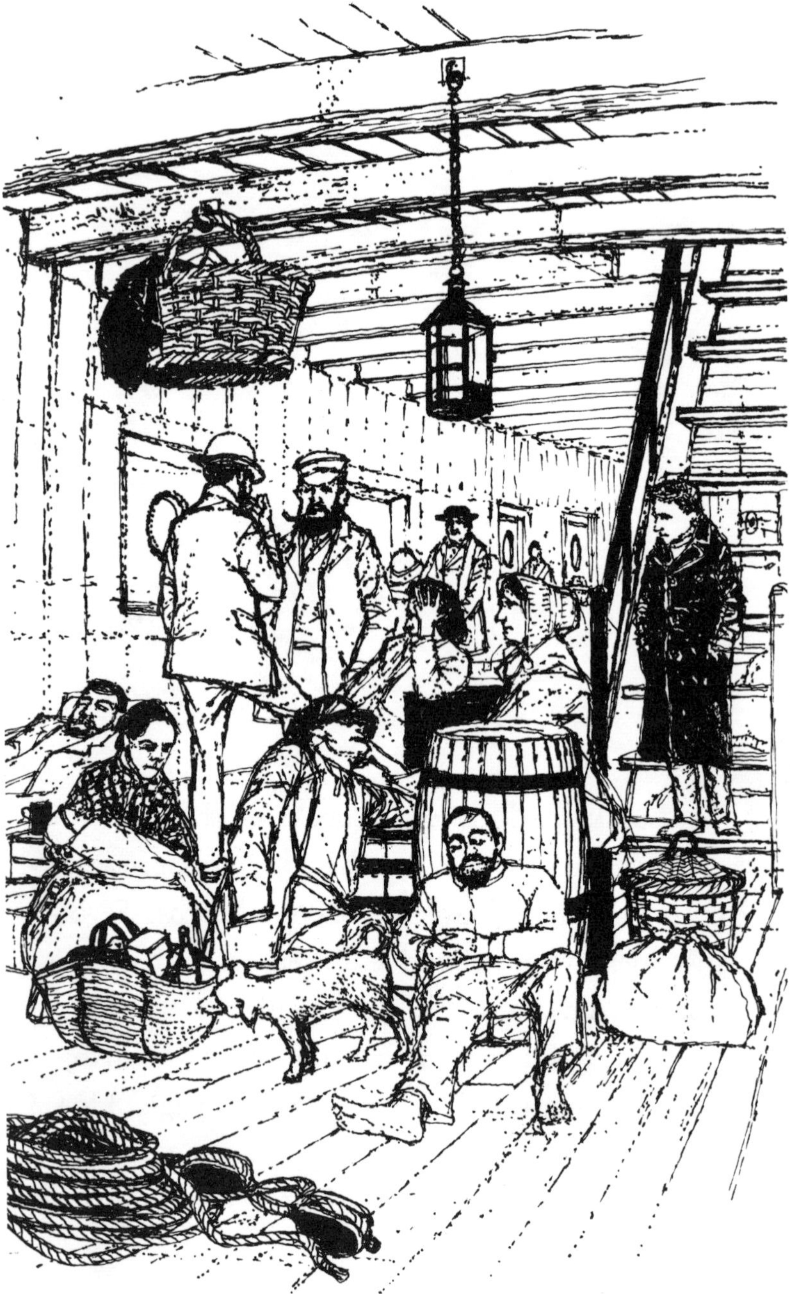

America

He had planned to learn English from Asmussen—English, the key to America—the very language he had not studied in school and now needed most. He would have long hours to discuss electricity as they paced the deck together. He would make friends with the small children he saw hiding behind their mother's skirts. He would win their friendship with his treasured locomotive.

Instead, Asmussen and most of the passengers spent the time in their bunks deep inside the ship, miserably seasick. But Karl was not seasick. He and one small boy ventured onto the deck together to watch a particularly rough storm. Karl, soaked to the skin, caught a very bad cold. His face swelled; his eyes were nearly shut.

On the day of landing, skies turned bright. White gulls flashed by as the ship steamed slowly into a calm harbor. A babble of excited voices brought Karl to the deck. All eyes were upon a giant figure, spikes rising from her head, right arm uplifted, holding a huge lamp. The Statue of Liberty! Karl had seen her picture on posters many times. Now here she stood—serene, impressive—all about her the shining water filled with boats, and behind her the buildings and steeples of New York City. Karl felt his spirits lift. America at last! Small tug boats guided their ship to the dock at Castle Garden where the Immigration office was located.

Asmussen told Karl, "Immigrants wait here for two days, and go before Immigration officials to be examined."

When the time came, Karl, wearing a tab with a long number hanging about his neck, stood before a man in uniform. The man frowned suspiciously when he saw Karl. He spoke curtly, "Profession?"

"Mathematicker," answered Karl timidly.

"Money?"

Karl pulled out some coins. "A few, Mr."

"Speak English?"

"A few."

"A job waiting?" Karl took off his spectacles and polished them. Asmussen, standing by, translated.

"Nein," answered Karl.

The man frowned again.

"No money. No job. No English. Deformed. Sick. You are undesirable. You can not enter. Step aside and go to the detention pen." He pointed to a huge sign in many languages over a door. "You will be shipped back."

Had Karl heard right? He stood frozen, unable to move, his heart thumping with fear. Go *Back?* Impossible!

Asmussen stepped forward, his face flushed.

"What," he shouted in a loud, excited voice. "You turn away a well-known scientist—one of the finest minds in the world? He will learn English. It will be child's play. Money, he certainly has. I am keeping it for him." Oscar pulled out the bills left from their steerage tickets. "As to a job, he goes with me. I have plenty of jobs. Also a rich uncle in America. I will take care of him."

The agent hesitated. He looked at the long line of laborers waiting their turn behind Karl, their families huddling over boxes and rolls of bedding. He shrugged his shoulders. "Brains we do need," he grumbled. "Ditch diggers we have plenty of. Proceed then."

He muttered to himself as he watched Karl and Asmussen leave the room. A strange picture, the big, Danish-American and the small, deformed dwarf. They walked side by side into the warm sunshine of Battery Park.

It was the year 1889, two months after the landing of the *La Champagne* at Castle Garden. Karl and Asmussen were sharing a room in Brooklyn. On this morning, Karl waited on a busy street corner in New York City. The shrill whistle of a blue-coated policeman in a tall helmet would give him a chance to cross the street. Horsecars rattled by, their bells clanging. He listened to the din and roar of the great city and looked up at buildings, which seemed very tall to him. His heart sang! At the shrill sound of the whistle, he crossed the street and hobbled quickly up the long stairway and into an elevated train.

This is my country, he thought. I belong here.

America

Soon, I shall take out naturalization papers. Karl August Rudolph Steinmetz, American citizen! He smiled to himself, then frowned. His name was so German! Would that sound right? I must talk it over with Asmussen, he thought.

There were many things to talk over with Asmussen each evening. His first job! He got it after only two weeks in America. But not as an engineer, as he had hoped.

"We have too many engineers already in America," he was told by pitying, curious clerks in the plants where he applied.

No, his job was as a draftsman, helping to draw plans for hat machinery. It took him two hours to get to the factory in Yonkers. At six o'clock each morning, Karl hurried from his small tenement room. He boarded a horsecar to the ferry, then an elevated train carried him from the ferry to the railroad station. By railroad train, he crossed the Bronx into Yonkers.

How lucky he was! On his salary of twelve dollars a week, he could easily support himself and even save a bit. Soon, he would be able to repay Asmussen the passage money. Already he knew enough English to get around alone. And what a friend he had in his new employer! Rudolph Eickemeyer, a tall, distinguished-looking man with a long, white beard, spoke German, was a refugee like himself, and was more interested in electricity than in hats. He had hired Karl after their long talk together about motors, dynamos, generators, and machines. More and more, Eickemeyer put Karl to work improving the electrical apparatus in the shop. This made Karl supremely happy.

He hurried home that evening to prepare a simple supper for two on the gas burner. Asmussen's voice boomed as he came in the door. "Karl —I have brought someone! A friend from your Breslau days. He wants to talk of old times and to hear of your life in America."

"Proteus!" With outstretched hand, a young German came to greet Karl. "Good to see you again, Proteus! How is the new job here?"

For long hours, the three talked over supper and after. As the visitor left, Asmussen said curiously, "Why does he call you Proteus? Where did you get such a nickname?"

Karl gazed at Asmussen, a light dawning in his eyes. Without replying, he limped across the room, picked up a pencil and wrote in small printlike handwriting:

Charles Proteus Steinmetz

He showed it to Asmussen with a merry smile. "My new name," he cried out, "which I shall use from now on in my new country. A good name for America. Also, it brings back the good memories of my life in Germany!"

That evening he wrote a long, affectionate letter to his father—his first from America. It was signed Charles P. Steinmetz.

7 ✳

First Discovery

Electricity is all about us, yet it can not be seen by the human eye. However, it can be used to produce a very bright light. Electricity is a form of energy which scientists have learned to control.

In the 1890's, houses and streets were dimly lighted. Most homes used smelly oil lamps or flickering gas jets. On the streets there were gas lamps that had to be lit each evening by a lamp

First Discovery

lighter with his long taper. There were a few arc lights, but these were too bright to look at and burned out quickly. Little was known about the uses of electricity. Thomas Edison, inventor of the light bulb, was trying to make a more practical one that would burn 40 hours and could be used indoors. Marconi was working on the idea of sending messages by electric waves. People everywhere were beginning to realize that electricity was a mighty power that could be harnessed.

Charles Steinmetz came to America at the beginning of this electrical age. It was fortunate for him. It was also fortunate that Rudolph Eickemeyer saw in him the genius which others overlooked. He realized that Karl's amazing mathematical mind would be wasted on ordinary, routine problems.

At first, Karl worked on the designing of motors for hat machinery. Then Eickemeyer freed him to work in the field which really interested both men, the use of electricity in machinery for industry. Karl began to design mo-

Steinmetz: *Wizard of Light*

tors for streetcars, water pumps, trolley cars, and elevators. But, at last, Eickemeyer decided to relieve him of all prosaic drafting chores.

"Charles, my electrical machines need constant repair, which is too costly. Find out why. Make a generator and transformer for me that does not get too hot and will not burn out. Make a motor with current that can be controlled. Experiment with the laws of electricity." So Eickemeyer gave Charles a goal. From then on, nothing could stop him from reaching it.

Joyfully, he began his first electrical research. He dug into the secrets and laws of this fascinating subject which had interested him from childhood. Such was his determination that he often forgot to eat or sleep, or to light the cigars that were constantly between his lips. It was mathematics he used to find the secrets in the coils of copper wire, the blocks of soft iron, the different kinds of electrical current. As he sat crosslegged on a chair in Eickemeyer's shop, he filled page after page with calculations.

"I must find a law that will help not only

First Discovery

Eickemeyer but engineers all over the world to design practical electrical machines," he told himself. Gradually, such a law began to form in his mind.

Eickemeyer continued to encourage him and, for three years, Karl worked on his law. Finally, he was ready to give it to the world. He belonged to the American Institute of Engineers, which he had joined soon after entering Eickemeyer's firm. Some of the greatest electrical engineers in New York City belonged to the Institute. Timid Karl did not speak out at the meetings. He listened, he thought, and he planned. But, finally, he was ready to read a paper.

It was very stormy that night of January 19, 1892. Karl put on his overshoes and rolled up his trousers. He wore his usual careless clothing; red cardigan jacket, shirt open at the neck. Painfully, he hitched himself up on the platform and began reading in his broken English. Not many understood him at first, but soon all fell under the spell of his great mind. Here was a man with

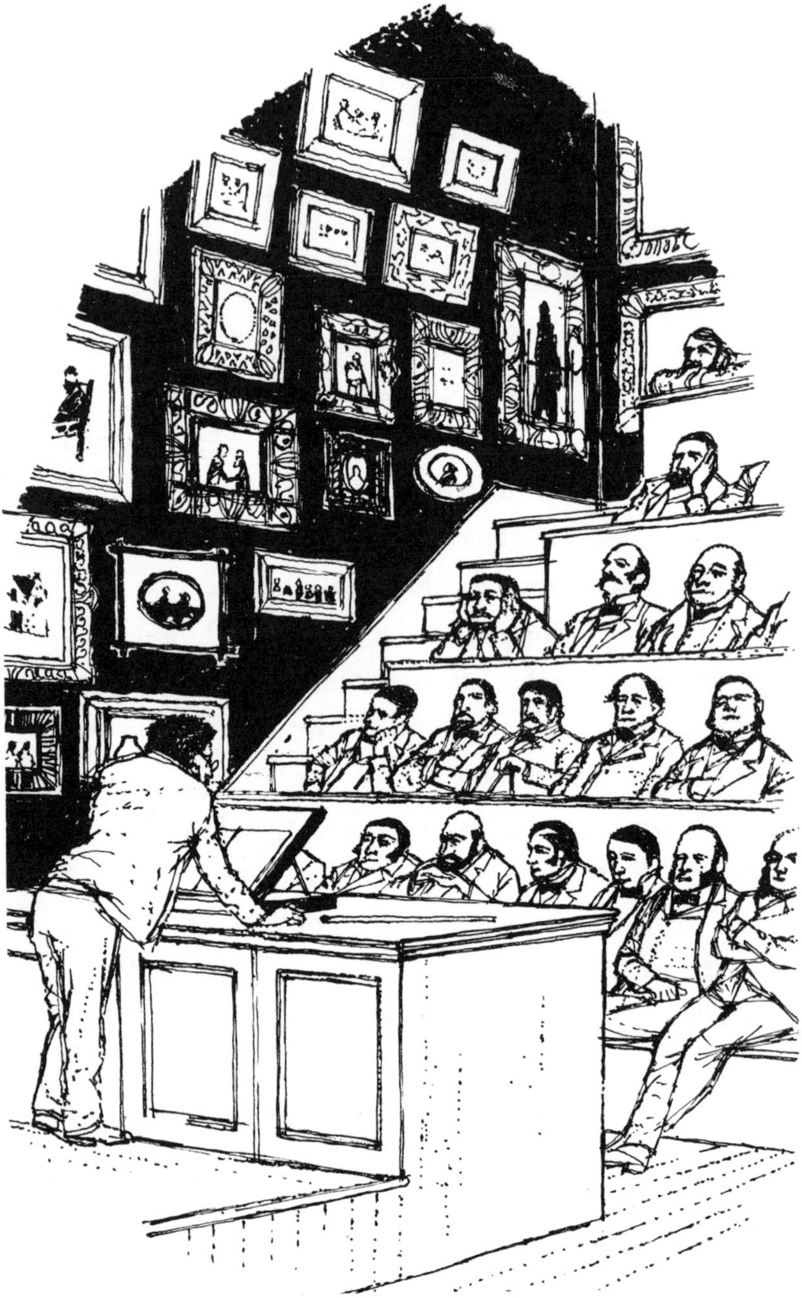

First Discovery

an important discovery! When he finished the applause and cheers were deafening.

Charles Steinmetz's discovery was not something that could be seen. Not for the eye to admire like a light bulb, a telephone, or a machine. It was for the mind; a law, a great general law, concerned with magnetism in the iron core of generators and transformers.

LAW OF HYSTERESIS

or

LAW OF MAGNETISM

The compass needle is a bit of magnetized steel. It has a north pole and a south pole. A bar of iron or steel placed inside a coil through which an electric current is flowing becomes magnetized. In most machines which use electricity, there is magnetized iron. Magnetism and electricity are forms of energy which can make things move.

In machines which use *direct current* (DC), the current flows in one direction and the magnetism does not change. In machines which use

Steinmetz: Wizard of Light

alternating current (AC), there is a reversal in the flow of electric current. When this happens the magnetic poles also reverse. The reversal of the poles does not take place instantly. The poles change quickly in soft iron and slowly in steel. The delay is called Hysteresis. One of the chief problems of the electrical engineer has been to calculate the period of delay, and to shorten the time as much as possible. Too long a delay can cause overheating and loss of efficiency.

Steinmetz's *Law of Hysteresis* was a mathematical law which enabled electrical engineers to calculate and reduce this loss of efficiency in the action of a machine.

Now engineers would know how much electric current to use in a motor. They would know what to expect from the electricity with which they worked. No more guessing; no more costly mistakes; no more burning out of insulation, thus ruining new machines. Steinmetz's Law of Magnetism or Hysteresis opened up tremendous new opportunities in industry, and was soon accepted and used in designing and drafting rooms

First Discovery

all over the country.

At the age of twenty-seven, Charles Steinmetz, a crippled dwarf, an immigrant, had become one of America's top-ranking engineers.

The publication of the law in magazines and newspapers over the country brought Steinmetz to the notice of an organization that was to become very powerful. This was the General Electric Company of Lynn, Massachusetts.

8

New Way of Life

"Charles Steinmetz is a wizard. We must get him for our laboratory." These words were spoken by Wilbur Rice, an officer and later the president of the General Electric Company. This company, formed in 1892, made all kinds of electrical equipment from light bulbs to dynamos. It had started one of the first electrical research laboratories in the United States. For this, the

New Way of Life

firm needed the best men in the field of electricity. They also wanted to buy up and control all available important electrical patents.

Rudolph Eickemeyer, the manufacturer who mixed hatmaking with electrical inventions, had what they wanted and needed. Eickemeyer dynamos and transformers were the best in the country, and Charles Steinmetz was known to be the man responsible for them.

Wilbur Rice lost no time in reaching Yonkers. At his first glimpse of Steinmetz in Eickemeyer's office, he stared hard. "Can this be the one I came to see?" he thought in alarm. The man was kneeling on a chair, his arms resting on its back. His hair hung down on hunched shoulders, and he smoked a long, thin cigar. Then Mr. Rice looked into twinkling eyes. He saw an eager smile and his doubts began to vanish.

When Steinmetz discussed physics, engineering, electricity, and mathematics, Mr. Rice knew that this was his man! But *The Wizard* refused to leave his friend Eickemeyer, the man who had given him his first job in America, even though he was offered a very large salary. He wished to remain where he was happy.

After Asmussen married his Swiss sweetheart and moved to Harlem, Steinmetz went to live in Yonkers with a man named Mueller, who worked at Eickemeyer's shop. Mueller had a wife and many children. Steinmetz loved children. Usually, after one glance, they ran from him. But the Mueller children grew to love him, and he could not bear the thought of leaving this jolly household.

At last, the General Electric Company decided to buy the entire Eickemeyer's firm. In this way, they hoped to get not only the services and genius of Charles Steinmetz, but the essential patents that Eickemeyer controlled. One clause in the contract was that Charles Steinmetz would join the General Electric Company. Eickemeyer could not resist the large price they offered and decided to sell his firm.

"Better for you, too," he told Steinmetz. "More opportunity." Urged by his employer, Steinmetz felt obliged to go to the new company.

New Way of Life

He left reluctantly and spent some very lonely months in Lynn, before the Company moved to Schenectady, New York. Here his fame and salary grew, but so did his loneliness. His life was at first a succession of dreary rented rooms, which later gave way to dreary rented houses, one after another. He tried to make himself at home in each house, but there was no family—no homemaker—to fill the emptiness.

Photographs of his father, sisters, and grandmother were on the walls of his study. Cigar butts and ashes littered the floor. Chairs were stacked with books. Boxes of sharpened pencils and reams of paper were piled against the walls. There were glass bowls of cigars and, in a prominent place, the little red locomotive!

Of course, Steinmetz always had a laboratory, in an alcove, or a basement, or a barn. It was cluttered with rolls and tangles of wire, transformers, batteries, and all kinds of electrical equipment. He constantly moved more and more equipment from General Electric to his home laboratory, spending even longer hours at work

Steinmetz: *Wizard of Light*

there, cooking meals on the lab stove, washing dishes along with beakers or test tubes.

As he grew more prosperous, Steinmetz spent thousands of dollars on plants and on animal pets. Out of his loneliness and from his need to love and be loved, he chose plants and animals that no one else might want. In one of the houses where he lived, a house on Liberty Street which he called Liberty Hall, he got permission from the landlord to build a glassed-in conservatory. It was on the right of the house, next to the barn which was his laboratory, and around it and the yard was a fence. He filled the greenhouse with huge, thorny, twisted cacti of a kind rarely seen. Snakes crawled among the cacti, and alligators and eels swam in the lily pond. Cages for sick monkeys and strange animals were crowded into the room in winter or were in the yard in summer. There was even a huge Gila monster from the Arizona desert. This creature with thick body, scaly skin, and fierce, ugly eyes allowed no one except its master to come near.

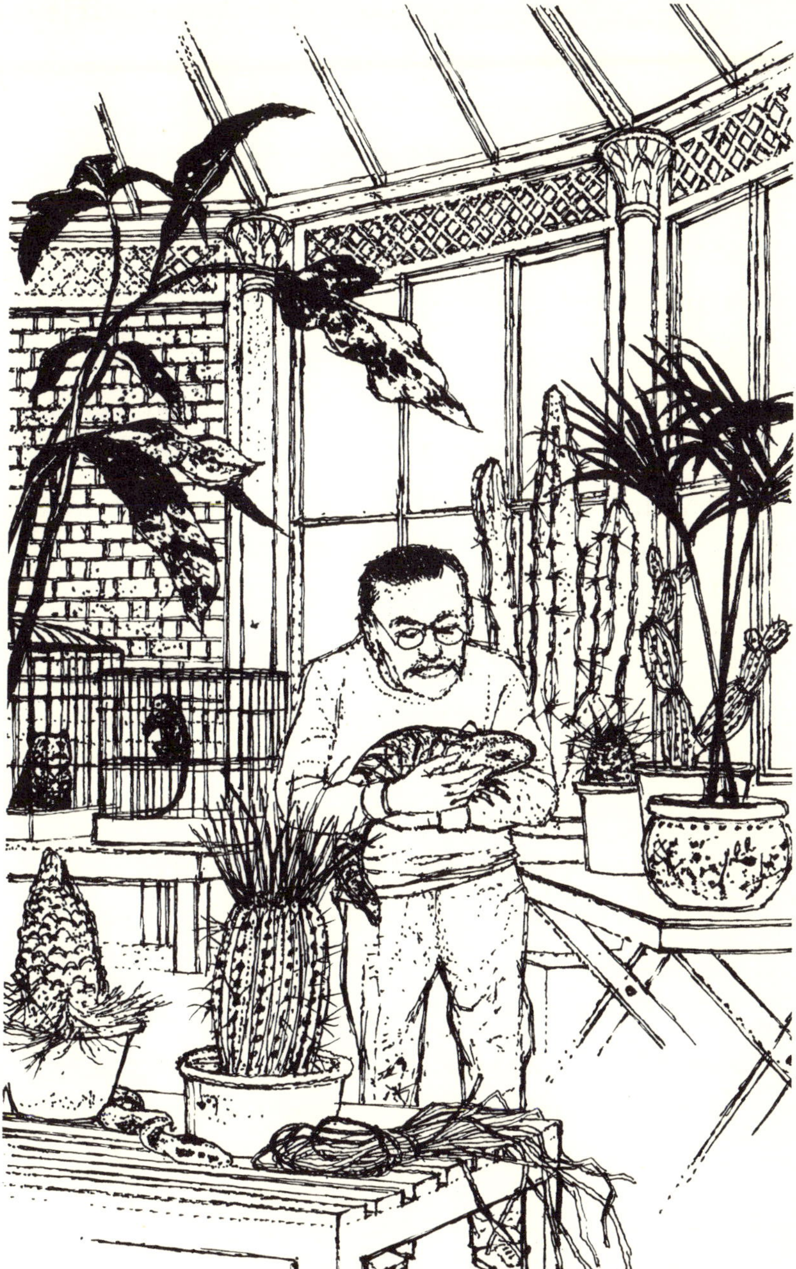

Steinmetz: *Wizard of Light*

People passing late at night often paused to gaze with sharp curiosity. They sniffed at peculiar odors and wondered at strange noises. Weird blue lights threw a glare over the deformed little man. With a long-spouted watering can, he watered ugly plants much larger than himself.

By day, children peered over the iron fence to catch glimpses of him and his animals as he stood in the yard. Sometimes, he talked to two pet crows perched on his shoulders. The crows lived in a tree in the yard and would always fly down at his whistle. Or the children might see him cradling the Gila monster in his arms, patting it as if it were a baby.

Steinmetz always waved and smiled when he saw the youngsters. They waved and smiled back. As eager for friends and fun and gaiety as in his Breslau days, he invited anyone in who would come. He gave weekly parties for his associates and assistants at General Electric, and he was as gleeful as a mischievous boy in his entertainment.

He wired his lab door and used old generators

New Way of Life

to cause sparks to fly from the doorknob. Visitors who sat down in his chairs received an electric shock from the wires beneath. Ladies glancing into the long hall mirror saw, to their horror, green skin and purple lips caused by a concealed overhead mercury lamp.

For eight years, Charles Steinmetz lived this strange life. During these years, he was advancing almost miraculously at General Electric, rising from a position as head of the Calculating Department to become Consulting Engineer with an unlimited expense account for apparatus and assistants, and an unbelievably huge salary.

But his landlords did not appreciate his mathematical genius. They objected to his use of their houses. Charred spots appeared on rugs and floors. There were dangerous explosions and unpleasant odors, and the possibility of fire breaking out. In 1900, this did happen. The barn laboratory at Liberty Hall burned to the ground. General Electric paid for the ruined building, but now Steinmetz had to move and build himself another workshop. So, he decided to build his own home.

9 ✳

Family Man

For many weeks, Steinmetz pedaled about on his bicycle, hunting all over Schenectady for a lot. At last, he found just what he wanted—a very sloping piece of land with a swampy bog on one side. It was property that no one else would buy and the puzzled agent sold it to him very reasonably. At once, Steinmetz began to plan.

First, he built the laboratory on the back of

Family Man

the lot. It was two stories high. On the second floor were two sleeping rooms. In one of them, he designed a bed made specially to fit his crooked body. The three rooms on the ground floor were equipped with plenty of work tables and electrical outlets. Low, wide shelves above the work benches were within easy reach.

It was at this time that Steinmetz met Joseph LeRoy Hayden. LeRoy was one of the "lab boys"—young men doing apprentice work at the plant. Steinmetz was experimenting, at his home laboratory, with an improved arc light. An arc light is an intensely bright, hot flame. It is formed when an electric current jumps a space between two conductors. The light is called an arc because it is curved like the arc of a circle. The two conductors between which the current flows are called electrodes.

Arc lamps, along with gas lamps, had been in use since 1877 for lighting city streets. But they were too intensely bright and the carbons used as electrodes burned out too quickly. Steinmetz had experimented with the use of magnetite—a

Steinmetz: *Wizard of Light*

hard, black, magnetic mineral composed of 72.4 percent iron—as a substitute for the carbon rods. Magnetite was more practical as it lasted longer and its bright bluish flame was less intense than that of carbon. The Steinmetz arc lamp was completed in 1900.

Steinmetz had asked General Electric to send him a man to help with this experiment. The young engineer who came was Hayden. Steinmetz liked him at once, liked his friendliness, his kindness, his efficiency. Most of all, he admired the young man's willingness to co-operate and to listen. Before long, he made a suggestion.

"Come live with me, Roy. It will cost you nothing, and I will teach you much. We can live in the laboratory until our new home is finished."

Hayden, proud to be working with a man of such fame, accepted readily. But he was amazed when Steinmetz showed him the house plans.

"My good friend," he cried. "The house is too big for two people!"

Steinmetz smiled, but kept his reasons to himself. Asmussen had left him when he took a wife.

Hayden might well want to do the same one day. A person must plan ahead.

The house was indeed huge. It took two years to build it. There was a big, airy living room with a stone fireplace and a huge doorway, a great kitchen which was well equipped, a library, and many large bedrooms, as well as a heated conservatory for his plants and animals. In an outdoor garden in the once swampy ravine, he planted iris, bordering clear pools of water. At last, it was finished. He and Hayden wandered about the big, empty rooms and admired them all. Then they returned to the laboratory to work long hours, to cook their steak and potatoes, and to sleep after work was over—just as they had done before the big house had been finished.

Soon after the completion of the house, Hayden married, as Steinmetz had foreseen. Strangely enough, he did not seem to mind that the couple found an apartment on the other side of town.

After the honeymoon, the young couple were just sitting down to their first dinner in their

Steinmetz: *Wizard of Light*

own home, when the doorbell rang. Hayden opened his door and there stood Steinmetz, apologetic, shamefaced, and eager. Of course, he was invited to share the meal, and the two men talked far into the night. This continued night after night for many weeks. Steinmetz realized that the young wife was displeased. The time had come. He must make his plea to Hayden's bride.

"Come to live with me," he begged. "My house is big. You may have it. Be the mistress of it. Furnish it as you wish, live as you will. Only the conservatory and a bedroom will be mine. I have needed and wanted a son and daughter badly. Don't take your husband away from me. Please!"

At first, Hayden's wife objected.

After several weeks, Steinmetz spoke to her again. She saw the deep longing in those blue eyes. She saw the frayed shirt collars and socks with holes at the heels. She saw the quiet, satisfying companionship that had grown up between Steinmetz and her husband.

"Will you promise to come to supper the very

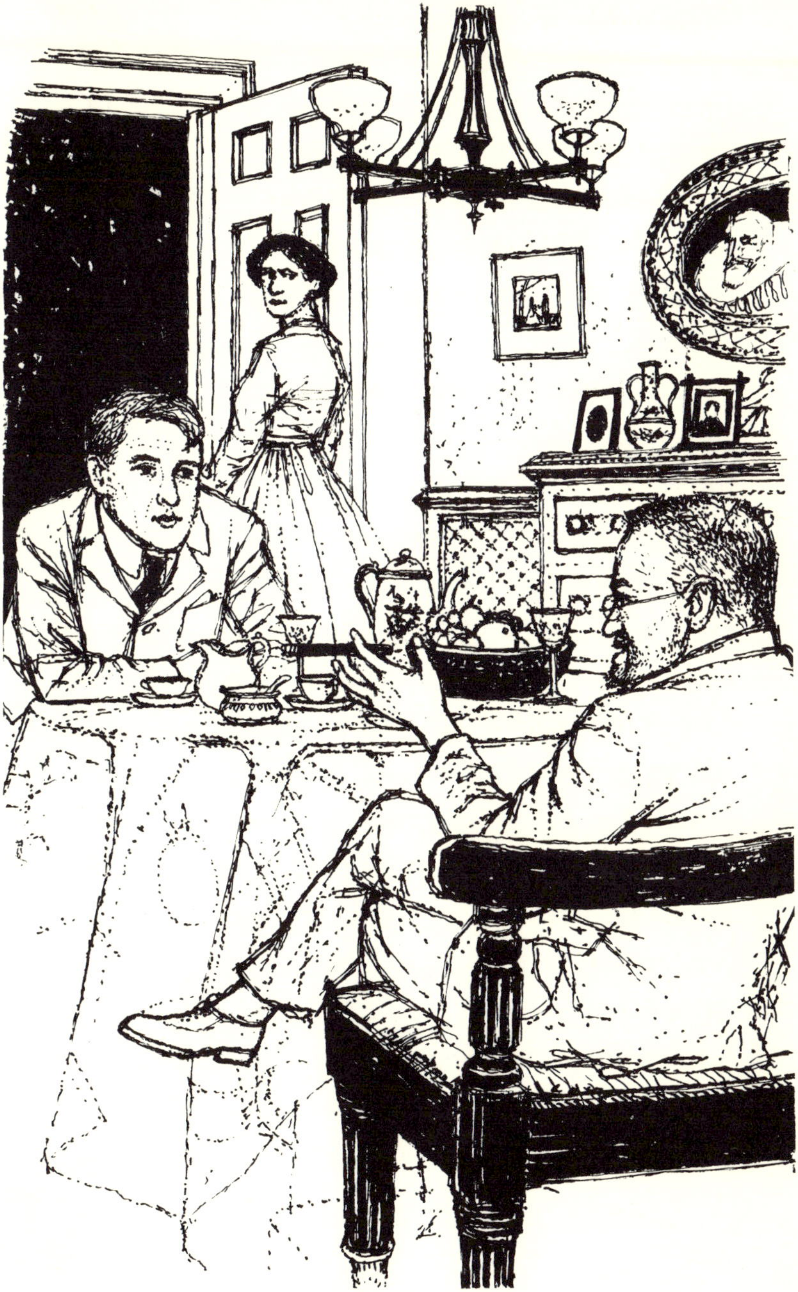

Steinmetz: *Wizard of Light*

minute I call you?" she asked, eyes twinkling.

"I promise. Oh, yes, I promise!"

"And not stay up all night talking to my husband but go to bed when I say?"

"Yes, yes, anything, whatever you wish I will do."

Laughing, Roy put an arm about the little man's shoulder. "All right, Dad," he said. "We'll move in tomorrow."

So, Charles Steinmetz found a home and family and began the happiest period of his life. A very satisfying and tender relationship grew up between them all. He adopted Hayden legally. The wife, whom he affectionately nicknamed "Mousie," became his daughter. Their three children were *his* grandchildren, whom he spoiled and on whom he lavished money and love. He curled himself in a big chair, before a crackling fire, and puffed his long cigar, carefully putting the ashes in a tray. He romped hilariously on the lawn with the children, and read them a bedtime story each night. He canoed with them down the quiet waters of the Mohawk River. He rocked the sick baby. He worked in the laboratory with his son. Charles Steinmetz was, at last, like other men. He had his own.

10 ✳

Years of Glory

"Good morning. Anything new for today, boys?"

Charles Steinmetz stepped through an open door of the Calculating Department at General Electric. With eyes alert and twinkling, hair ruffled from his morning bicycle ride, he stood for a moment. He puffed furiously on a long cigar.

Young men, bending over engineering problems on their desks, paused and looked up. But no one spoke. A few men raised their hands in a respectful morning salute or nodded their heads, smiling. They watched as Steinmetz shuffled quickly across the room and into a small office. It bore the sign "Consulting Engineer."

" 'The Supreme Court,' " whispered an engineer to a new assistant. The man looked puzzled. "That is what Dr. Steinmetz is called here at G. E. He is the boss, the Wizard who solves and settles problems no one else can work out. He understands and explains laws only he knows."

"He must get a good salary," exclaimed the assistant.

"Some say one hundred thousand dollars a year! No one really knows."

The newcomer gave a long whistle. Then he grinned, and pointed to a large sign: NO SMOKING. "What about that law up there? The Doctor didn't seem to have noticed that one!"

The engineer chuckled. " 'The Supreme Court' made a decision on that law, too. He told G. E., 'No smoking, no Steinmetz.' So they let him have his way. He smokes as much as he wishes. He is too valuable to lose."

Steinmetz: *Wizard of Light*

Steinmetz had brought fame and fortune to General Electric and to himself. During those first lonely years in Schenectady, he had been given a place as head of the Calculating Department—a job for which he was not well fitted. He did not like to direct other men. The paper work which was required to organize and check the reports of others seemed unnecessary and tiresome to one who could solve the most complicated engineering problems in his head. So, General Electric made him Consulting Engineer.

He held this position for the rest of his life and as the scientific "Supreme Court" he was in his glory. He left his new home and came into the office for only two or three hours a day to hold conferences, or for an appointment when some staff member needed help. The rest of his time was spent in the laboratory experiments which he loved, with unlimited freedom to work where and when he wished, and to buy all the equipment he needed. So, in deep contentment, he pored over his experiments and laws, turning

Years of Glory

all the results over to General Electric.

Great ideas came constantly from his great mind, which could not stop working. Turbines, generators, dynamos, transformers, and cable lines had always filled his thinking. He knew that his Law of Hysteresis would be of little value unless alternating current could be put into general use. This is the electrical current which is called AC. In the 1890's, only direct current was used in machines and in generating systems. Direct current cannot be transformed into high voltage and thus transmitted efficiently to great distances away from the plant where it is generated. Steinmetz knew that, unless a formula for the use of alternating current could be worked out, the long distance transmission of electricity would be impossible.

He made many seemingly useless experiments but from the signs and symbols that filled Steinmetz's notebook, there came at last new rules and formulas. He designed a new and more powerful transformer, one that would work under all conditions, that could raise the voltage in the cable lines, and that could transmit electricity over long distances. The Law of Hysteresis had solved one major problem in the field of electricity. Engineers were able to calculate the loss of electric current in a motor and thus prevent costly machines from being ruined. Now, the Law of Alternating Current had solved a second problem of the long distance transmission of electricity. From this investigation into the field of alternating current, there came later, patents for more than fifty types of electrical apparatus. From this investigation came also the publication of his book on alternating current which remains one of the classics of electricity today.

By 1901, Steinmetz had become world famous through his Law of Alternating Current. Honors began pouring in upon him. He was made president of the American Institute of Electrical Engineers, where he had so long attended meetings and had been too timid even to speak. He had never received a college degree, but in 1902, Harvard University, at an impressive ceremony,

Years of Glory

gave him an Honorary Master of Arts Degree. His citation read: "The foremost electrical engineer in the United States and therefore in the world." Union College of Schenectady in 1903, gave him a Doctor of Science Degree, which he had earned in Breslau fifteen years before. They invited him to be a Professor of Electrical Engineering and head of that department. General Electric allowed him to do this and, for ten years, he had two jobs, although he never accepted pay from Union College. Now he was both Doctor and Professor. And because of his interest in children, the Board of Education in Schenectady made him their president.

Friends filled his life now. People on the streets still stared at him but no longer with pity. They forgot his deformity in their admiration and all who really knew him loved him.

Important men, sometimes from abroad, in top hats and tail coats, streamed to his laboratory, to meet him and to talk with him. Often, he was out. Sometimes they found him at his summer camp in the Mohawk Valley.

· 89 ·

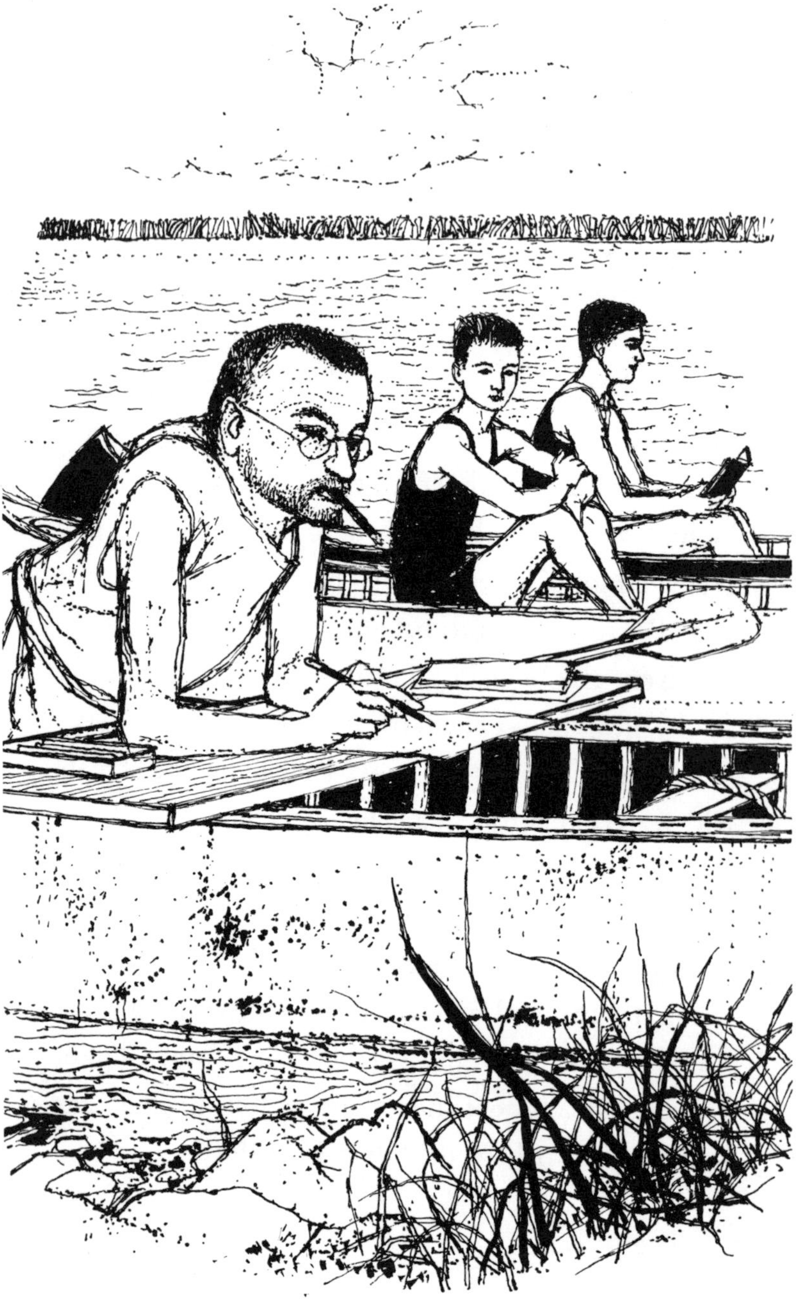

Years of Glory

Floating near the shore, in the shallows of the Mohawk River, they would see him in his canoe. The tiny boat with its small double paddles had been bought for his grandchildren. Kneeling on a pillow on the bottom, he hunched over notebooks—pencils, and cigars spread out on a board over the gunwales. Steinmetz drifted and worked and smoked for hours at a time.

Barefoot, and dressed in a faded red bathing suit, he would come smiling to meet his visitors who had made the long climb down through the brush to find him. He would offer to cook them his favorite dinner of steak and potatoes.

Einstein, Edison, and Marconi were among the distinguished guests. With Einstein, he talked mathematics by the hour. With Marconi, he discussed radio waves and transformers. But he could not talk to his good friend Edison, who was very deaf. So, to Edison's delight, he tapped his conversation on the inventor's knee in Morse Code. Steinmetz had studied the code to please a grandson.

Light, electricity, magnetism—all one energy.

Steinmetz: Wizard of Light

Steinmetz loved to play as well as work with these phenomena! All around the outside of his big home he installed the giant magnetite lamps which he and his son had developed, and which were the first successful street lamps in the United States. Inside his conservatory and laboratory, he experimented with the mercury vapor lamps which he had installed in Liberty Hall. His grandchildren delighted in the cold, blue-green light which made his plants even more ghostly. They delighted in all his experiments with light —the sparkling firecrackers he made for them— all his tricks and pranks. They were always saying, "Make us more magic, Daddy Steinmetz, more magic."

In his later years, he became interested again in a childhood fascination—the power of lightning. The cross country wires made possible by the use of alternating current were targets for lightning. Often, whole power lines were wrecked. He made an intensive study of the subject, traveling and observing. An idea took shape in his mind.

"People call me magician and wizard," he told himself. "I must do something magical and spectacular. Something that people everywhere can understand and see with their eyes."

11 ✻

Dreams Come True

It was the year 1921. Steinmetz was growing old. His most important work had been done. He had become a bit vain. He was proud of being called a magician and a wizard by the press, proud that many people stood in awe of him.

Scientific experiments still filled his days. But now, he began to play more and more with them. He began to plan ways in which he could stir

Dreams Come True

the imagination of the public.

His camp in the Mohawk Valley helped him accomplish this. The one little room perched high on the cliffs was struck by lightning and almost completely destroyed. Instead of being dismayed, the Wizard was jubilant! This was what he had long wanted—to be able to observe with his own eyes the habits and effects of lightning. He hastened to his camp and poked about in the debris. He took many pictures, made measurements, and jotted down endless calculations.

He studied the path of the bolt from the tree through the window to the metal lamp, through the wiring system to a large mirror which lay shattered in hundreds of bits. Ah, this may prove to be the evidence I must have, Steinmetz thought.

Dropping to the floor, he began piecing the bits together. For days, he toiled at this almost impossible task. His goal accomplished, he carefully placed and sealed the mirror between glass plates. Then he took it home to his lab. On the silvered back of this treasure was traced the evi-

Steinmetz: *Wizard of Light*

dence he needed—the path of the bolt. From it an exciting plan came to him!

He would make a lightning machine that could hurl bolts of electricity! Destructive bolts like the one which had hit his camp. These were the ideas he had confided to Edison. Now he would be considered as great as Edison. He would prove himself the magician that they thought him to be. But how could he release such power? One hundred thousand volts! He had no condenser large enough to store and release so much energy.

He bought new apparatus for his laboratory in Schenectady. He built an odd-looking, high-voltage lightning machine to generate electricity. It held racks of thick plate glass—200 of them in all. Each plate was covered, top and bottom, with foil and held together by heavy copper bars. High-voltage transformers charged these plates, which acted as condensers, to a very high voltage.

On a table made of a copper plate, Steinmetz set up a toy village. It had brightly painted houses, a school, stores, and a white church with

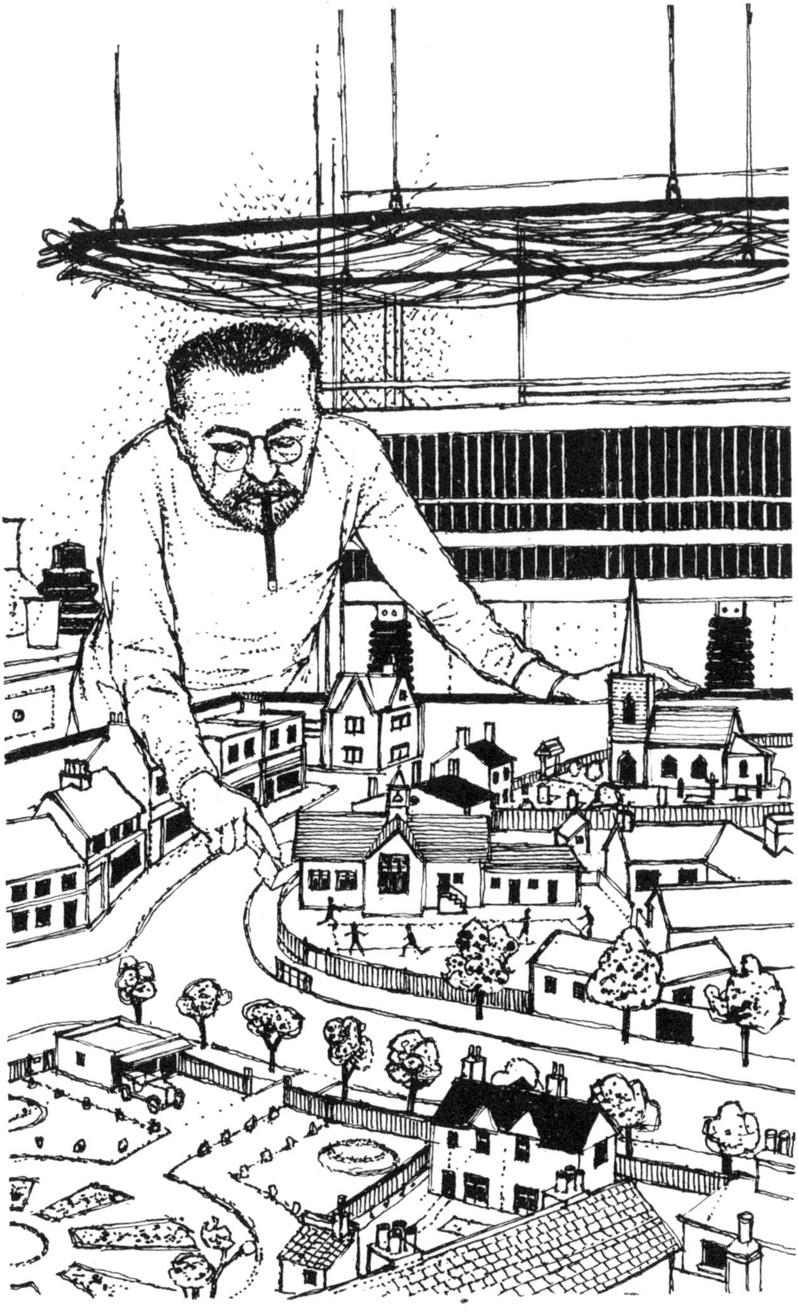

Steinmetz: Wizard of Light

a tall, white, metal spire. Artificial trees lined the walks, children played in the schoolyard. Above the gay little village was suspended a mass of heavy wire. All was ready.

Invitations went out to great scientists, to news reporters, and to officials of General Electric. On a springlike day in the winter of 1922, these important people poured into his laboratory. They sat behind the wire screening which marked the "danger line," shifting uneasily in their seats. The wait was tense, exciting!

"The glass condenser plates and the wire above the village set up conditions similar to a thunder storm," Steinmetz explained. "Electric charge is produced by the high-voltage machine. The charge builds up on the plates in the same manner that raindrops carry electricity into clouds. The condensers will store and release the charge in a shaft of lightning powerful enough to kill a man. This will strike the village from the wires above."

He pressed a switch behind him. A strange humming noise filled the room. A glow appeared in the generator tubes. On and on went the

Dreams Come True

steady, nerve-wracking hum as the condenser plates became charged and slowly filled. Then, suddenly, there was a rumbling crash, a blinding flash of light shot from the wires above, and the tall spire of the little church crumbled. Dense smoke filled the air. Steinmetz snapped off the switch and everyone rushed to the table. There was no village!

Everyone turned to praise and congratulate Steinmetz, who was smiling happily. He had proven himself the Wizard! At once, his picture, with that of his lightning machine, appeared on the pages of every newspaper in the land. But Steinmetz had a reason in back of his startling spectacle. Before the year was out, there came a practical result from his experiment—the first lightning arrester adequate for wide commercial use.

By experimenting with artificial lightning, he could now develop generators and transformers and transmission wires which could be made lightningproof. He could control the vast voltage of the bolt so that it would jump harmlessly from the service line to the ground.

This saved whole systems of power lines. It saved thousands of dollars for power companies. For Steinmetz, it resulted again in a flood of invitations to speak all over the country. He accepted the request of the Western Branch of the American Institute of Electrical Engineers. They arranged a speaking tour for him. Steinmetz set forth to tour the West, taking along his son and his entire adopted family. "I won't go unless the children come, too," he told Roy.

People were curious to see and hear the little man of whom they had read so much. Even when he talked on such subjects as high-voltage insulation or engineering problems of the future, they came by the thousands. Not only scientists but the public as well. In city after city, he spoke to crowds packed into the auditoriums. It did not matter whether they understood the important words. The once-rejected little immigrant had become an idol to his fellow countrymen.

His son often reproached him for overtiring himself. He always replied, "Roy, I must pay the

Dreams Come True

debt of gratitude I owe my country and justify the honors which it has heaped upon me."

Hollywood, where he was the guest of Douglas Fairbanks, the movie star, was a great thrill. He and the actor liked each other at once. He limped along beside the tall, powerfully-built man, went with him to wild west shows, and studied the machinery of the motion picture industry. "The movies offer new uses for electricity," he told Fairbanks excitedly.

He returned home at last, his mind filled with ideas, supremely happy over his "vacation." "Our next family trip will be to Europe," he told Hayden.

Back in Schenectady, he suddenly felt very weak. The tour had been hard on a man whose health had always been frail. He could scarcely walk from the train to the taxi. His son helped him into the house and into bed.

He never left his room after the cross-country trip. Always happiest when with his family, he was content to stay quietly in his bed in the big bedroom, sometimes reading scientific literature

Steinmetz: *Wizard of Light*

or filling page after page of his notebook with tiny figures. He talked and joked with his grandchildren who spent part of each day at his bedside. Death was gentle for the little dwarf. It came on October 26, 1923, on a bright, sunny, fall morning. After a cheerful conversation with his son, he closed his eyes to rest. When the breakfast tray was brought in, the light had gone out.

Flags were at half-mast on the schools of Schenectady on the day of his funeral. People of all ranks came to pay their respects; scientists, electricians, General Electric officials, reporters, governors, and individuals. Telegrams poured in to the family.

No well-known invention bears the Steinmetz name. He helped perfect the devices of other men. Among these were the lamps that turn night into day on our city streets, electrifying our nation, and the lightning arrester which protects that electrification. He improved generators, turbines, and cables. He created man-made

Dreams Come True

lightning, but he was not merely an inventor. Neither was he an ordinary scientist.

His work was on paper. The results of his vast knowledge, far beyond the comprehension of ordinary men, helped solve the problems of other scientists and engineers. They accepted that knowledge and his formulas and put the laws to work on actual apparatus in the growing factories of our nation.

Without Steinmetz, electricity would be far less useful than it is. Through his Law of Alternating Current, he helped solve a part of the baffling riddle of electricity once and for all. He taught the world how to harness, control, and increase electrical power—how to send it by wires over long distances, over hills, valleys, and streams. To Steinmetz must go the credit for the use of every machine that operates on alternating current! The electric locomotive that hauls trains, electric cranes, machinery in coal mines, on farms, in steel mills, rolling mills, and factories are all the result of his fertile mind.

In our homes, the electrical devices which are

Steinmetz: *Wizard of Light*

so much a part of our daily lives—the electric toothbrush and shaver, toaster and iron, fan and air conditioner, electric typewriter, stove, washing machine—all operate on alternating current, which makes them cheap enough for almost everyone to buy.

All of us can be grateful to the "little dwarf with the giant mind." In spite of handicaps not of his own making, he helped bring about changes in the way people live. Remarkable changes for his country, America—the land that Charles Proteus Steinmetz chose and loved.

Index

alternating current (AC), 66, 87, 92, 103-104
Alternating Current, Law of, 88, 103
American Institute of Engineers, 64-65, 88, 100
arc light, 77-78, 102
Asmussen, Oscar, 48-59, 70

Breslau (Germany), 3

direct current (DC), 65, 87

Edison, Thomas, A., 61, 91, 96
Eickemeyer, Rudolph, 57, 61-63, 69-70
Einstein, Albert, 91
electricity, 59-67, 87-88, 101, 103, see also lightning

Fairbanks, Douglas, 101
Fechner, Professor, 19-23

General Electric Company, 67-102

Harvard University, 88-89
Hayden, Joseph LeRoy and family, 77-83, 100-102
high-voltage transformers, 96-99
Hysteresis, Law of, 65-67, 87-88

invisible ink, 44

Index

La Champagne, 51-53, 56
Liberty Hall, 72-75
lightning, 17, 19, 92-99, 102-103
lightning arrester, 99, 102
lightning machine, see high-voltage transformers
Lux, Heinrich, 43-46

Magnetism, Law of, see Hysteresis
magnetite lamp, 77-78, 92
Marconi, Guglielmo, 61, 91
Math Society, 36, 41
mercury vapor lamp, 92
Mohawk River Valley, 82, 89-91, 95
Mueller family, 70

"Proteus," 35-37, see also Steinmetz, Charles P.

Rice, Wilbur, 68-69

Schenectady Board of Education, 89
Socialist Club of Breslau, 42-45
St. John's School for Boys, 16-32
Steinmetz, Charles P. (Karl August Rudolph Steinmetz):
    early childhood experiments, 3-14
    pre-university education, 14-32
    college years, 33-46
    flight from Germany, 46
    Switzerland and America, 47-57
    first job, 57
    new name, 59
    early work with electricity, 61-63
    formulation of Law of Hysteresis, 63-67

Index

    joins G.E., 67-70
    naturalist interests, 72-74
    new home and family, 76-83
    Consulting Engineer at G.E., 84-88
    honors and degrees, 88-89
    artificial creation of lightning, 92-99
    summary of contributions, 101-104
Steinmetz, Clara, 6, 12-16, 26
Steinmetz, Grandmother, 3-15, 23, 26
Steinmetz, Karl, 5-48
Steinmetz, Marie, 6, 12-16, 26
"Supreme Court," 85-86, see also Steinmetz, Charles P.

The People's Voice, 43

Union College of Schenectady, 89
University of Breslau, 33-47

About the Author

Anne Guy is the author of some ten books for children. Born in Hannibal, Missouri and educated first at a Normal School, Mrs. Guy received her B.A. only a few years ahead of her son at Maryland University. A former teacher, Mrs. Guy now lives in Chevy Chase, Maryland.

A Note on the Type

This book is set in Garamond, a modern rendering of the type first cut in the sixteenth century by Claude Garamond (1510-1561). He was a pupil of Geoffroy Tory and is believed to have based his letters on the Venetian models, although he introduced a number of important differences. It is to Garamond that we owe the letter that we know as Old Style. He gave to his letters a certain elegance and a feeling of movement which won for their creator an immediate reputation and the patronage of the French King Francis I.